Contents

City of the Dead

CENTRE:
The Great Fire of London of 1666, which swept through the City of London for four days.

As people hurry past London's oldest churches, little may they realize what lies beneath them. Many have crypts and undercrofts – vaults or stone chambers used as chapels or burial places – and these reveal centuries of London's dead. Most of the crypts in England were built during the Norman period (1066–1154) and the years since then have added to the numbers of bodies. It is not unusual to find a family crypt or vault on private estates, particularly among royal families.

RIGHT:
The cloisters of St Bartholomew the Great; the church was originally an Augustinian priory.

RIGHT:
Busy porters at Smithfield Meat Market, 1870.

One of London's oldest churches is St Bartholomew the Great in West Smithfield, founded in 1123 as an Augustinian priory. Flanked by St Bartholomew's Hospital and Smithfield Meat Market, it was at the heart of a densely populated district for many centuries. Mary Tudor drank wine and ate chicken in the gatehouse while watching Protestant martyrs burn at the stake. Amazingly, the church survived the Great Fire of 1666, Zeppelin raids in the First World War and bombs during the Blitz of the Second World War. The crypt, under the Lady chapel at the east end of the church, was used as a charnel house (a vault or building storing human skeletal remains) and is where priors and monks were buried. In 1895 the crypt was made into a mortuary chapel for the use of the inhabitants of the crowded courts and alleys near the church.

Little Ann Lemaistre was buried in 1763 in a lead coffin which preserved her bonnet and dress – she was only three and half months old. Hers was only one of 984 skeletons discovered (of which 20 per cent were infants and children) when the crypt of Christ Church Spitalfields became the first post-medieval burial vault to be investigated by archaeological methods in the late 20th century. The crypt, which runs under the entire length of the church, was used for over 1,000 burials between 1729 and 1852. Architect Nicholas Hawksmoor (1661–1736) designed six churches in the City of London, the first of which was Christ Church Spitalfields, built between 1714 and 1729.

When the crypt of St Andrew Holborn, which dates back to AD 951, was excavated about 1,800 lead and wooden coffins, some from the 15th century, were discovered. Those working on the site, including archaeologists from the Museum of London, had to be vaccinated against the risk of smallpox. This was a highly infectious and usually fatal disease, and very common until wiped out in the 19th and 20th centuries. Some of the coffins in the crypt contained the bodies of influential people buried before 1831, such as Attorney-General Sir Edward Coke, who prosecuted the Gunpowder Plotters in 1606.

BELOW: This early engraving of 1597 shows how near the church of All Hallows by the Tower was to the scaffold on Tower Green.

All Hallows by the Tower is the oldest church in the City of London, and Roman and Saxon stonework and artefacts are still to be seen in the crypt. Following execution on nearby Tower Hill, numerous beheaded bodies were brought to this church, including Thomas More, Bishop John Fisher and Archbishop Laud. William Penn, founder of Pennsylvania, was baptized in All Hallows and in 1666, when it was threatened in the Great Fire, the building was saved largely through the efforts of Penn's father, Admiral Penn. John Quincy Adams, sixth President of the USA, was married here in 1797. The church, which was heavily bombed in 1940, has a museum containing portions of a Roman pavement.

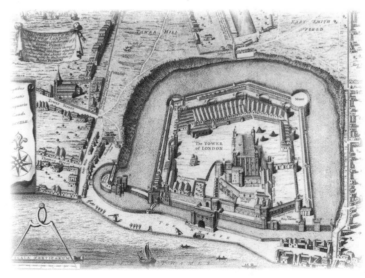

RIGHT:
An Edwardian painting of St Clement Danes in the Strand.

An easy church to spot is beautiful St Clement Danes which stands in the middle of the Strand outside the Royal Courts of Justice. The church was completed in 1682 by Sir Christopher Wren and it now serves as the central church of the Royal Air Force. It is named after the earliest church on the site, which was founded by descendants of the Danish invaders. Between 1569 and 1853 many people were buried in the crypt, and in 1956 their remains were cremated and the ashes reinterred under the South Stair. A chain hanging on the crypt wall was used to secure the coffin lids against body-snatchers – a common problem. Walk carefully down the spiral stairs leading to the crypt chapel where plaques commemorate many of those who were buried here, particularly Protestants fleeing persecution from abroad.

Near the glittering wealth of Hatton Garden, where gold, silver and diamonds are traded daily, is St Etheldreda's, the oldest Catholic Church in England. In the 16th century, Sir Christopher Hatton, Lord Chancellor and close friend of Elizabeth I, occupied the land and gardens at an annual rent of £10, ten loads of hay and a red rose. During his tenancy, part of the undercroft

Oranges and lemons

St Clement Danes is claimed by some to be the St Clement's in the nursery rhyme *Oranges and Lemons* (' … say the bells of St Clement's'). However, St Clement Eastcheap also makes a similar claim.

RIGHT:
The crypt of St Etheldreda's, where 18 bodies were discovered in 1873.

Body-snatching

Body-snatching was the secret removal of bodies from their graves to sell for dissection or anatomy lectures in medical schools. Such medical schools have always needed – and still do need – a steady supply of cadavers. Before the Anatomy Act of 1832, the only legal supply of corpses for this purpose was those of prisoners, often guilty of heinous crimes, condemned by the courts to death and dissection. Such sentences did not provide enough bodies for the medical and anatomical schools: while during the 18th century hundreds were executed for trivial crimes, by the 19th century only about 55 people were hanged each year. Yet, with the expansion of medical schools, as many as 500 cadavers were needed annually. Before electricity could power refrigeration, bodies would decay rapidly and become unusable. Therefore the medical profession turned to body-snatching.

of the church was used as a tavern, with drunken brawls often interrupting the services above. The crypt was repaired in 1873 and during the digging some bodies were discovered. These were the victims of a tragedy in 1623, when a number of Catholics gathered in secret at the French Ambassador's house in Blackfriars to hear a special sermon. Tragically the floor of the room collapsed and over 100 were killed. Given the strong anti-Catholic feeling at the time they had to be buried in secret: 18 of them were interred at St Etheldreda's and are here to this day.

St Bride's Fleet Street fell victim to the Great Fire of London in 1666 and the medieval church was destroyed. A new church was completed in 1703 when Sir Christopher Wren's high steeple was finished and which has provided the inspiration for wedding cakes ever since! At 69m (226ft), the steeple is the second tallest of Wren's London churches, with only St Paul's being higher. When Wren designed the church he built it over the remains of six previous churches with extensive burial crypts. In 1854 the crypts were sealed up, but when they were later opened they revealed hundreds of skeletons which gave an insight into 1,000 years of history of the site. Lead coffins can still be seen in the crypt.

ABOVE: Body-snatchers raiding a cemetery to provide a cadaver for dissection – an illustration by the famous 'Phiz'.

LEFT: St Bride's Fleet Street during the London Blitz in December 1940, when the church was gutted. It was later rebuilt.

In the heart of the City of London the impressive Guildhall has been the centre of civic government for hundreds of years. It contains several historic buildings dating back to the 15th century, including the hall, large medieval crypts, the old library and the print room. It is still the ceremonial and administrative centre of the City of London and its Corporation, and as such dates back to the 12th century. Famous trials have taken place in the hall including those of Lady Jane Grey and Thomas Cranmer – both were executed for their 'crimes'. The medieval crypt beneath the Guildhall is the most extensive in London. The west crypt, which may be part of a late 13th-century building, burned in the Great Fire of 1666, when it completely collapsed. However, it was extensively restored and is now in use again.

Lambeth Palace, on the south bank of the River Thames opposite the Houses of Parliament, has been the London residence of the Archbishops of Canterbury since the 13th century. Nicolas Pevsner described the Crypt Chapel as 'one of the best preserved medieval vaults in London'.

'Turn again, Whittington!'

The famous city church St Mary le Bow has become synonymous with its old curfew bell. To be born within the sound of Bow bells is the traditional definition of a Cockney. In 1392 Dick Whittington was reputed to have heard Bow bells call him back to London to become Lord Mayor. Dating from the 11th century, St Mary le Bow has the first arched crypt to be found in any church in London, thus making it one of the capital's oldest and most important standing stone structures. Showing great resilience, it survived the Great Fire of London and so was incorporated into Wren's church of the 1670s.

The vaulted undercroft and chapel were completed around 1220 – although the crypt was first used as a storage area for beer and wine. After the main chapel was destroyed during the Second World War, the crypt was used instead. In 1966 Pope Paul VI gave as a gift the fresco of 'Christ in Glory', which now hangs on the wall of the crypt. This gift marked a real milestone: the first official meeting between the Archbishop of Canterbury and the Papacy since the 16th century.

Near Trafalgar Square is the superb church of St Martin-in-the-Fields. An older church dating from 1222 stood here when the area was 'in the fields' – the countryside between the cities of Westminster and London. The present church, which was designed by James Gibbs and completed in 1726, was London's first free lending library in 1860 and also had the first church service broadcast in 1924. The vast crypt, which runs almost the whole length of the original building, now houses the popular Crypt Café. At the top of the stairs to the crypt is a stone which records how in 1773 the vestry ordered that, 'no Graves be Dug in any of the Vaults of the Church as a Practice thereof will be Prejudicial to and in time Endanger the Foundation'. The following year another order stated that any corpses buried in the vaults under the church must be 'in Leaden Coffins'! During the Second World War Ed Murrow, the famous radio journalist, broadcast news of the Blitz to America from the steps of St Martin-in-the-Fields. Describing the scenes of chaos and quiet in London he commented, 'it's a beautiful and lonesome city where men and women and children are trying to snatch a few hours' sleep underground.'

ABOVE: The popular Crypt Café at St Martin-in-the-Fields.

BELOW LEFT:
The memorial to Lord Nelson in the crypt of St Paul's.

BELOW RIGHT:
The memorial to Florence Nightingale.

St Paul's Cathedral sits proudly on the highest point of the City of London and is one of the capital's most visited sights. The present cathedral was designed by the court architect Sir Christopher Wren and built between 1675 and 1710 after the earlier church was destroyed in the Great Fire of London. The crypt is the largest in Europe with over 200 memorials, and is the resting place of some of the nation's greatest heroes, poets and scientists. Lord Nelson lies at the centre of the crypt, directly below the centre of the dome. He was interred beneath the black sarcophagus made for Cardinal Wolsey in the 16th century. The Duke of Wellington rests on a simple casket of Cornish granite. The Iron Duke left a colourful list of namesakes: Wellington boots, the dish Beef Wellington, a brand of cigars, several ships, a school and several towns around the world. Sir Christopher Wren, architect of St Paul's and many other City of London churches, is buried in his cathedral, surrounded by members of his family. Other notable memorials are to artists Sir Joshua Reynolds and Sir John Everett Millais; scientist Sir Alexander Fleming, who discovered penicillin; composer Sir Arthur Sullivan and sculptor Henry Moore. There are also effigies and fragments of stone that pre-date the cathedral.

Footprint

The crypt of St Paul's is, unusually for a cathedral, the exact 'footprint' of the cathedral floor above.

The present church, begun by

Westminster Abbey is the traditional place of coronation and burial of English and British monarchs. The present church, begun by Henry III in 1245, is a treasure house of paintings, stained glass, pavements and textiles. There are over 3,000 people buried in the church and cloisters, and more than 600 monuments and memorials. Among these are royal effigies of Edward III, Henry VII and his queen, Elizabeth of York, Elizabeth I, Charles II, William III, Mary II and Queen Anne. The Pyx Chamber (1070), one of the oldest parts of the abbey, is a low vaulted room which was used as a repository in the 13th century. In 1303, while the king was away in Scotland, the treasury of the Wardrobe was burgled with money and plate stolen. The Abbot and monks of Westminster were suspected of the robbery and sent to the Tower of London. However, they were later released and one Richard de Podlicote and his associates were hanged for the crime. The present double oak doors at the chamber entrance were fitted after this and the room went on to be used for storage of valuables from the Exchequer. There are two large chests dating from the 13th and 14th centuries, which were made in the room. The chamber's name comes from the wooded boxes – pyxes – which contained samples of the realm's coinage before being tested for purity in the Palace of Westminster.

A walk along Magpie Alley near Fleet Street will amply reward the visitor with a view of the remains of a 14th-century Carmelite medieval crypt which lies beneath the street. It was once the Whitefriars Priory which stretched from Fleet Street to the River Thames and contained a church, cloisters, garden and cemetery. In the Middle Ages the medieval crypt offered sanctuary for thieves, murderers and prostitutes afraid to enter the priory. The White Friars were founded on Mount Carmel (now in Israel) in 1150, but were driven from the Holy Land by the Saracens in 1238. Henry VIII dissolved the priory in the middle of the 16th century and the buildings eventually fell into disrepair.

ABOVE:
Westminster Abbey's magnificent west front.

LEFT:
The Pyx Chamber at Westminster Abbey.

ABOVE:
The Circle of Lebanon catacombs in Highgate Cemetery.

RIGHT:
The grave of Emmeline Pankhurst at Brompton Cemetery. The sash tied around the grave is in the colours – purple, green and white – of the Suffragette Movement.

Although burial grounds were already in existence long before the 19th century, the first public cemetery in London was opened in 1833 in Kensal Green. Others followed over the next 14 years and made up the 'Magnificent Seven': Norwood (1837), Highgate (1839), Nunhead (1840), Abney Park (1840), Brompton (1840) and Tower Hamlets (1841). These Victorian places of rest became well known for their elaborate gravestones, vaults and catacombs. Highgate, the most famous, has the impressive Circle of Lebanon catacombs, a structure of 20 sunken tombs. Kensal Green has brick vaulted catacombs with space for 10,000 bodies.

Peter Rabbett and friends

Author Beatrix Potter, who lived near Brompton Cemetery, took names from the headstones – such as Mr Nutkins, Mr McGregor, Jeremiah Fisher, Tommy Brock and even a Peter Rabbett – for many of her characters.

In 1995 Brompton Cemetery opened its catacombs for the first time since 1911 to reveal some 1,200 rotting Victorian coffins. (The gates had been originally closed in 1911 to stop thieves from stealing human skulls and bones.) Among the famous that rest in Brompton are Emmeline Pankhurst, the suffragette, Samuel Cunard, founder of the Cunard Line, and John Wisden, author of the cricket almanac.

Bunhill Fields, a former dissenters' graveyard in Islington, dates back to the site of a Saxon burial ground. It was originally called Bone Hill after more than 1,000 cartloads of human bones from the charnel house in St Paul's Churchyard were dumped here in 1549. Bunhill Fields developed rapidly as a cemetery and was popular with nonconformists and dissenters such as John Bunyan and William Blake. Around 120,000 bodies are buried here and 2,500 monuments survive.

Do come in ...

For one weekend in September each year Open House takes place when over 1,000 buildings in London open their doors free of charge. It is a wonderful opportunity to visit places that are not normally open to the public.

West Norwood Cemetery had over 164,000 burials – including Mrs Beeton, the cook, and Sir Henry Tate, sugar magnate and founder of the Tate Gallery – in 42,000 plots as well as several thousand interments in its catacombs. The catacombs were constructed with a hydraulic catafalque (a raised platform, often movable) to lower coffins from the Episcopal Chapel to the vaults. A single-pump hydraulic lift was installed in 1839 and could swivel to make unloading the coffins easier.

Action Stations!

RIGHT:
The Map Room of the Cabinet War Rooms, exactly as it was left in 1945, complete with wax models.

RIGHT:
Churchill's bedroom at the Cabinet War Rooms.

A number of military citadels exist under London, most dating from the Second World War and the Cold War. They were mainly used for communications, military purposes and civil defence. So complex is this network that it is uncertain as to what extent the tunnels are linked together. There are certainly miles of these tunnels built under central London stretching below Whitehall, Leicester Square, Holborn and Victoria.

The Churchill Museum and Cabinet War Rooms are centrally located beneath the Treasury at the junction of Horse Guards Road and Great George Street. They are dedicated to the life of Sir Winston Churchill and the fascinating network of rooms is almost unchanged since they were abandoned in 1945. The rooms originally served as the secret underground headquarters that were the nerve centre of Britain's war effort. When Churchill visited the Cabinet War Rooms in May 1940 he stated, 'this is the room from which I'll direct the war'. The Map Room,

THE X FILES
I WANT TO BELIEVE

CINEMA   EMPIRE   CASINO

which was left almost exactly as it was when its doors were closed for the final time, was of such importance to Churchill that his own room was immediately next to it with an adjoining door. The complex was constructed in 1938 with cellars 3m (10ft) beneath the ground reinforced with concrete. Inside is a deeper level called 'The Dock' which is a warren of very low cramped corridors and rooms that were used as sleeping quarters for all but senior staff. With the problem of rats, lice, lack of flushing toilets and noise from the air system, it was clearly an unpopular place for most of those working here who, understandably, preferred to take their chances above ground with the bombs. The section open to the public is only a part of a much larger facility that originally covered 1.2 hectares (3 acres) and included a canteen, hospital, shooting range and dormitories.

The Cabinet War Rooms in Whitehall had two tunnels built during the war extending north and south to connect with the Government's Rotunda citadel near Millbank. The Rotundas, which were designed to withstand the impact of a 227-kg (500-lb) bomb, were three buildings occupying a site around Great Peter Street and Marsham Street, and were demolished in 2003. The south tunnel from the Cabinet War Rooms extends to government offices in Marsham Street and, although now disused, it is rumoured to emerge in the basement of Westminster Hospital. The older north tunnel connects the Cabinet War Rooms with the government telephone exchange in Craig's Court near Charing Cross Station, where there is another complex system of tunnels.

ABOVE:
Leicester Square today: many miles of tunnels run under this area.

Beneath our streets

There are several rumoured escape tunnels from Buckingham Palace which are said to run under Green Park, the Piccadilly and Victoria Underground lines, and Wellington Barracks. Whether this is true or not, during the Second World War the royal family did have access via a tunnel to a fortified suite of rooms beneath Curzon Street in Mayfair.

RIGHT:
Churchill in 1940, giving his famous V-sign.

Another secret bunker, deep enough to be bomb-proof, was Paddock, the codename for an alternative shelter to the War Rooms, built in Neasden at the start of the Second World War. Designed to accommodate the War Cabinet and 200 staff, it was intended to be a last refuge in the event that the Battle of Britain was lost. Churchill only used it once, partly because of its distance from the City and the fact that it was damp. The operation room still exists 21m (70ft) beneath the surface.

BELOW RIGHT:
The switchboard at the Kingsway Telephone Exchange.

BELOW:
Green Park, under which it is rumoured there are escape tunnels from Buckingham Palace.

Possibly the most important post-war military citadel in Britain is Pindar, a bunker beneath the Ministry of Defence in Whitehall. Authorized by Prime Minster Margaret Thatcher as a command centre during the Falklands War, it became operational on 7 December 1992 with its main purpose to provide the Government with a protected 'crisis management facility'.

Kingsway Telephone Exchange was over 30m (100ft) below High Holborn and Chancery Lane. It was built as a deep-level shelter in the 1940s to protect 8,000 people. However, it was eventually used by a section of MI6 known as the Inter Services Research Bureau, part of the Special Operations Executive originally set up to help resistance movements in Nazi-occupied Europe. After the war the tunnel area was extended and it became a 'city under the City' during the Cold War, providing the most secure telephone exchange in Britain which included air conditioning, a water supply, a restaurant and a fully stocked bar. In 2008 this secret twilight zone was put up for sale and the warren of tunnels was almost emptied of equipment.

Q-Whitehall

Rumours of a communications facility under Whitehall referred to as Q-Whitehall has circulated for many years although its existence has never been officially confirmed or denied. It is said to run under Whitehall from Trafalgar Square to King Charles Street.

LEFT:
Looking south from Trafalgar Square down Whitehall, the rumoured site of Q-Whitehall.

'A vast monstrosity'

The Admiralty Citadel is London's most visible military citadel. It was constructed in 1940–41 with foundations 9m (29ft) deep and a concrete roof 6m (19ft) thick. Churchill described the building as a 'vast monstrosity' and not surprisingly ivy now covers it in an attempt to hide its ugliness. An eastbound tunnel stretches under the Ministry of Defence while another extends in the direction of Pall Mall.

From the outbreak of the Second World War in 1939 long-suffering Londoners used the London Underground as air-raid shelters. In 1940 eight Underground stations – Belsize Park, Camden Town, Goodge Steet, Stockwell, Clapham North, Clapham Common, Clapham South and Chancery Lane – had deep-level air-raid shelters built underneath. Above the ground, pillbox structures were erected to protect the shelters' shafts from bombs going further underground. These pillboxes contained lift machinery and spiral staircases. The shelters had two parallel tunnels about 3,657m (12,000ft) in length. The Government originally used the shelters, but with the intensifying of flying bombs (V1s and later V2s), five of them were opened to the public in 1944. After the war Goodge Street shelter continued to be used by the Army until the 1950s. The Chancery Lane shelter was converted into Kingsway Telephone Exchange and later expanded to serve as a Cold War government shelter.

D-Day

Goodge Street Underground station became the headquarters of General Eisenhower, Supreme Commander of the Allied Forces in Europe, and it was from here on 6 June 1944 (D-Day) that he broadcast the announcement of the invasion of France.

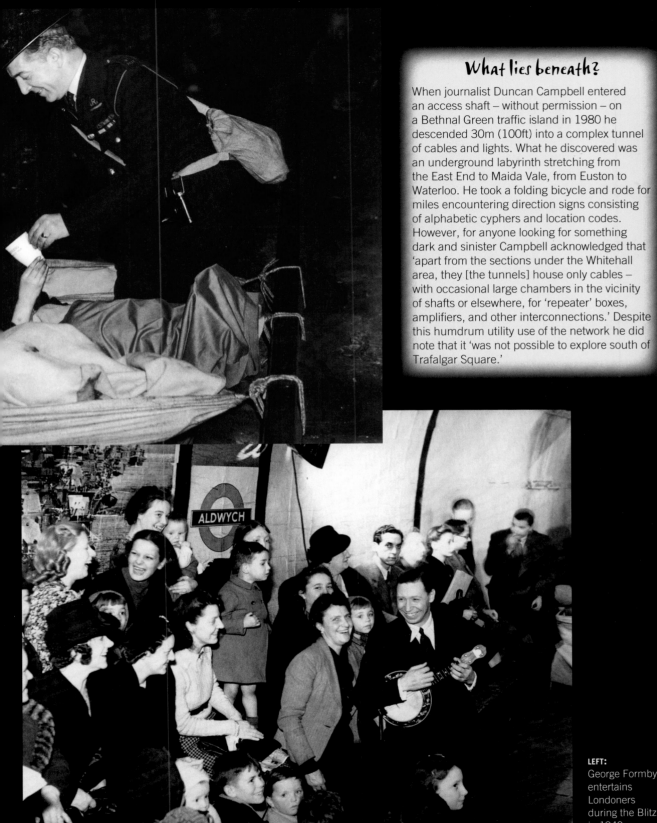

What lies beneath?

When journalist Duncan Campbell entered an access shaft – without permission – on a Bethnal Green traffic island in 1980 he descended 30m (100ft) into a complex tunnel of cables and lights. What he discovered was an underground labyrinth stretching from the East End to Maida Vale, from Euston to Waterloo. He took a folding bicycle and rode for miles encountering direction signs consisting of alphabetic cyphers and location codes. However, for anyone looking for something dark and sinister Campbell acknowledged that 'apart from the sections under the Whitehall area, they [the tunnels] house only cables – with occasional large chambers in the vicinity of shafts or elsewhere, for 'repeater' boxes, amplifiers, and other interconnections.' Despite this humdrum utility use of the network he did note that it 'was not possible to explore south of Trafalgar Square.'

LEFT: George Formby entertains Londoners during the Blitz in 1940.

Murder Most Foul

London has a particularly violent and grisly history with its executions, tortures, floggings, pillories, prisons, violence, murders and blood sports. In addition there was disease, plague, awful living conditions, pollution, smog and dreadful sanitation.

Among the very early displays of cruelty and barbarism was the Roman amphitheatre where people watched brutal fights between gladiators and wild animals. The bloodier the battle the more the crowd cheered. Today, London's historic Guildhall includes the best library on London history, an impressive crypt and an art gallery. But beneath the art gallery lies the important 5,000-seater Roman amphitheatre – the only one in London – discovered by Museum of London archaeologists in 1988. Two thousand years ago this was the site of much gory entertainment. In the 4th century St Augustine described a visit to the arena: 'the whole place was seething with savage enthusiasm … in the course of the fight some men fell; there was a great roar from the whole mass of spectators.'

When the Romans left Britain in AD 410 their amphitheatre lay derelict for hundreds of years. London eventually became a prosperous trading centre and by 1065, when Harold was crowned in Westminster Abbey, London was the largest and most important city in England. Public displays of barbarity continued throughout the history of the capital to uphold law and order. The London Dungeon entertains and scares tourists with its history of various tortures since the medieval period, albeit in a 'gallows humour' style. The cellars of the dungeon are located under London Bridge Station and contain ghoulish attractions, many accompanied by smells and cries of agony.

BELOW:
Be very afraid! One of the many scary attractions at The London Dungeon.

Other exciting discoveries beneath the City include a 2nd-century Roman forum and basilica under Gracechurch Street. Roman bath houses in Huggin Hill (fed by a natural spring) and Milk Street have also been found. Perhaps the most exciting 20th-century Roman discovery in London was the Temple of Mithras (the Roman god of heavenly light) in Walbrook. Inside the temple were fine marble likenesses of Minerva and Mercury. Below what is now the Merrill Lynch Financial Centre another rare statue of Minerva (the Roman goddess of arts, crafts and war), remnants of the Roman London Wall and a medieval bastion have been discovered. In AD 200 Londinium (the Roman City of London) was surrounded by a huge wall with a fort in the north-west corner. The wall stretched for over 3km (nearly 2 miles), stood 6m (20ft) high and was 2.4m (8ft) thick at the base. In 1969 archaelogists found eight dog skeletons on the eastern part of the old wall, in the area now called Houndsditch. The remains of the wall's west gate can be seen beneath the streets next to the Museum of London.

Her Majesty's Tower of London has witnessed countless imprisonments, torture, trials and executions. Traitors' Gate, with its wide arch, was a frequent route into the Tower from the river, when the Thames was more of a highway than it is at present. Earlier known as the White Gate, it was found convenient as a landing place for prisoners who had been tried at Westminster. Sir Thomas More, Queen Anne Boleyn, Thomas Cromwell, Earl of Essex, Queen Katharine Howard, Thomas Seymour, Duke of Somerset, Lady Jane Grey and Princess (later Queen) Elizabeth were brought by barge under London Bridge, where the heads of recently executed prisoners were displayed on pikes. They passed under the arch of the gate on their way to meet their fate in prison or on the scaffold. In the crypt under the Chapel of St John some of the Tower's bloodiest secrets are revealed: several inscriptions carved by prisoners who took part in Wyatt's rebellion in 1554, the execution axe dating from the 1660s, the block used at the execution of Simon, Lord Lovat in 1747, instruments of punishment used for confining prisoners and a model of the rack as it existed in the Tower in 1809.

Across the road from The London Dungeon are The London Bridge Experience and London Tombs. Located under the streets, The London Bridge Experience shows, through special effects, animation and realistic characters, what life was like in days gone by. It displays a 2,000-year history of London Bridge, complete with haunted tunnels. The tombs, where human remains and historic artefacts have been discovered, is for the brave-hearted and is designed to scare those who enter, with its haunted catacombs and unsavoury creatures that leap out from the darkness. Look out for the ghost of Emily!

Clink Prison Museum on Bankside is built on the foundations of one of the original prisons once owned by the Bishops of Winchester. The word 'clink' is believed to have derived from the clinking of the manacles, fetters, chains and bolts as well as meaning 'in prison'. The Clink was in use from the 12th century until 1780. Life in the prison was grim and the prisoners were treated badly with beatings and torture as common practice. In 1485 bishops were ordered by Henry VII to incarcerate priests in the Clink for adultery, incest and fornication whilst Mary I used the Clink to imprison and starve Protestants. Elizabeth I continued to use the prison for religious persecution, but this time it was mainly Catholics who were on the receiving end. Special stocks and a ducking stool were installed in the cellar. The present museum recreates the conditions of those times with a series of cells, a whipping post, torture chair, foot crusher and other torture instruments.

Headless ghost

Anne Boleyn's ghost is said to haunt a basement in Durham House Street, where she lived in her last weeks. The house where she resided has long gone but the cellar survives.

CRAZY TIMES!

ABOVE: The block used for the execution of Lord Lovat in 1747, the last person to be beheaded on Tower Hill.

LEFT: The pillory, a common punishment in Georgian England.

The cellars of the nearby Hop Exchange in Southwark, where hops from Kent were originally traded for brewing, cover an underground area of nearly 0.5 hectare (1 acre), and are reputed to have been part of the old Clink Prison.

While exploring the House of Detention at Clerkenwell, an old Middlesex County holding prison, a number of people have had the feeling that they are not alone. Many have caught sight of a shadowy figure moving swiftly through the darkness ahead of them. Others have heard the heart-rending sobs of a little girl who, it is believed, is lost and wandering the dank maze of corridors and passageways. Children were imprisoned here and the distress they suffered must have been terrible. It is also rumoured that an unsavoury individual stalks women who wander alone through the maze of tunnels.

There was a prison here from 1616, although the early building was demolished in 1890. This left a labyrinth of underground passageways dating from 1844. During the London Blitz the basement, originally used for the reception of prisoners, medical examinations, baths and kitchens, was re-opened as an air-raid shelter.

The cellars of public houses might not be the sort of places one associates with old prisons but the Viaduct Tavern, the Morpeth Arms and the Mason's Arms have such stories.

The Viaduct Tavern – the last example of a late Victorian gin palace left in the City – is opposite the Old Bailey, standing near the site of the infamous Newgate Prison, notorious for its squalid conditions. Across the road is the church of St Sepulchre-without-Newgate, where the clerk would toll a handbell (which can still be seen in the church) outside the condemned man's cell just before his execution, to warn him. Beneath the Viaduct are prison cells, the remains of the old Giltspur Street Compter Prison, demolished in 1855. They are reputed to be haunted.

LEFT:
The Morpeth Arms, which served the warders of Millbank Prison.

'Your money or your life!'

The famous Spaniards Inn at Hampstead, built around 1585, has a tunnel that is said to have been used by the notorious highwayman Dick Turpin on a number of occasions when he was eluding pursuit.

Newgate was the most notorious prison in England where executions were a regular feature. The last public execution took place outside its walls in 1868 although hangings continued within its walls until 1902. Prison reformer Elizabeth Fry wrote in 1813, 'I have lately been twice to Newgate to see after the poor prisoners who had poor little infants without clothing, or with very little and I think if you saw how small a piece of bread they are each allowed a day you would be very sorry.' Although the prison is long gone there is still a tiny passage behind the wall at the end of Amen Court that was named 'Dead Man's Walk', where prisoners were led to their executions. Some 97 condemned men are buried beneath the stone flags of the corridor that connected the prison with the adjoining courts next door.

The Morpeth Arms on Millbank was built in 1845 to serve the wardens of the huge and forbidding Millbank Prison. In 1849 the Millbank area was described by Charles Dickens in *David Copperfield* as a 'melancholy waste … A sluggish ditch deposited its mud at the prison walls. Coarse grass and rank weeds straggled over all the marshy land.' The fortress-like building consisted of a warren of complex tunnels, long, dark, narrow corridors, twisting passages and deep cells that stretched underground as far as the Morpeth Arms. A notice in the pub records that a 'labyrinth of underground passages and cells known as "the dark" are still in evidence'.

The Mason's Arms is a short walk from Marble Arch, the location of Tyburn gallows, and claims to be on the site of the dungeons where prisoners were held before they were hanged. The present pub cellar is reputed to have a tunnel that ran from the dungeons to the gallows and has the original vaulted arch where evidence of manacled chain fittings can be seen.

ABOVE:
An artist's impression of the highwayman Dick Turpin.

One of the most grisly affairs concerns that of Enon Chapel, built around 1823 just off the Strand. As the congregation worshipped in the upper part of the chapel they were oblivious to the dreadful happenings that were going on down below. In 1839 a gruesome discovery was made in the 18-m (60-ft) long, 9-m (29-ft) wide vault. Thousands of corpses had been packed into the vault over a 20-year period: the work of a corrupt Baptist minister who had been providing burials for a bargain fee of 15 shillings (75p) per body. So crammed in were the corpses that worshippers were inhaling the noxious fumes of rotting flesh, as well as witnessing hundreds of bug-like insects flying about the chapel. The minister had tried to get rid of some of the human remains by mixing them with loads of mingled dirt and then throwing them into the Thames on the other side of Waterloo Bridge. In 1848 a surgeon by the name of George Walker bought the chapel and, at his own expense, had the bodies removed to Norwood Cemetery.

BELOW:
The Strand in the 19th century, near the Enon Chapel.

ADELPHI THEATRE

RIGHT:
Jack Cade's Cavern, 1833.

The case of Enon Chapel was not an isolated incident. St Martin's Ludgate, St Anne's Soho, St Clement's Portugal Street and a number of others were guilty of similar practices. The gravedigger at St Clement's said that the ground was so full of bodies that he could not make a new grave. This scandal led in part to the reform of burials in London in the mid-19th century.

In Victorian times caverns on Blackheath, created as a result of quarrying, were used for parties and balls. The 49-m (160-ft) deep caverns were fitted with chandeliers, a bar and a ventilation system. However, the caves were closed in 1854 when the lights went out at a masked ball and people panicked. The caves were also gaining a rather saucy reputation. They became known as Jack Cade's Cavern, named after the rebel leader who assembled an army of 5,000 peasants on Blackheath in 1450 to protest against the unfair taxes and weak leadership of Henry VI.

Mole Man

The 'Hackney Mole Man', William Lyttle, had been burrowing since the 1960s from his Victorian property. He hollowed out a web of tunnels and caverns spreading up to 20m (65ft) in every direction from his house. On one occasion the whole of the opposite street lost power after he tapped into a 450-volt cable. It took a court order in 2006 to temporarily evict him in order to enable engineers to fill the holes with cement, at an estimated cost of £100,000 – for which 75-year-old Mr Lyttle was billed. He told *The Guardian* newspaper that he 'first tried to dig a wine cellar, and then the cellar doubled, and so on.'

LEFT:
The Camden Catacombs.

Stables below the streets

Beneath the busy streets of Camden close to the Roundhouse, lies a labyrinth of tunnels known as the Camden Catacombs. These were built in the 19th century as stables for horses and ponies that worked for the railway delivering and picking up goods.

Eat, Drink and Be Merry

Not surprisingly there are countless cellars in London, many dating from medieval times. They have had various uses including the storage of wine, beer, ammunition, cold meat, ice, silver and laundry. Many are still used for these whilst others have been converted to serve other purposes.

THE MADMAN HIMSELF !

In 1698 the Palace of Whitehall was the largest palace in Europe with over 1,500 rooms. It was also the residence of English and British monarchs from 1530 until 1698 when it was destroyed by fire. A surviving part of the original palace is the Tudor brick-vaulted wine cellar (known as Henry VIII's wine cellar), 21m (70ft) long and 9m (30ft) wide which is located under the present Ministry of Defence building in Whitehall. After the Second World War the cellar was relocated 3m (9ft) to the west and nearly 6m (19ft) deeper. This huge operation was carried out without significant damage to the structure – or the wine.

A more modern working cellar is that of Berry Bros & Rudd, wine merchants of St James's Street, founded in 1698 and still one of Britain's best wine merchants. Their extensive cellar stores up to 18,000 cases of wine. Anyone wishing to have a wine-tasting experience would enjoy a visit to Vinopolis, which is built into massive Victorian railway arches near London Bridge and has a small amphitheatre for wine-tasting sessions.

LEFT:
Wine-tasting
at Vinopolis.

Along Chancery Lane are the London Silver Vaults, the world's largest retail collection of fine antique silver where dealers still trade. The Chancery Lane Safe Deposit was opened in 1876 with the purpose of renting strong rooms mainly to safeguard the silver, jewellery and personal documents of London's wealthy elite. The silver vaults start at 'the big door' on the third floor below street level, with each dealer housed in individual thick vaults similar to those of a bank.

MPs' wine supply

One of the country's finest wine collections is housed in a cellar in the vaults of Lancaster House, off the Mall, and serves the needs of MPs in the House of Commons. The cellar contains approximately 39,500 bottles at an estimated value of £792,000.

LEFT:
Some of the glittering wares at the London Silver Vaults.

RIGHT:
There has been a pub on the site of Ye Olde Cheshire Cheese for several centuries.

BELOW CENTRE:
American author Mark Twain drank at Ye Olde Cheshire Cheese.

BELOW:
Charles II is said to have used the tunnel connecting the Nell of Old Drury pub with the Theatre Royal opposite.

Cellars and vaults make ideal places for cafés, bars and nightclubs but let's not forget that other type of subterranean escape – the public toilet. There are too many to list here but one example of how an Edwardian convenience was transformed into a place of entertainment is members-only Ginglik, located underneath Shepherd's Bush Green. This very public convenience was originally built to serve the needs of visitors to the 1908 Olympic Games at nearby White City. The toilets were converted in 2002 into a bunker venue that hosts live music, comedy, club and cabaret nights thus giving a new meaning to the term 'watering hole'.

Many tunnels connect buildings, usually churches and pubs. These tunnels have often given rise to stories based on fact as well as speculation. The London Apprentice pub at Isleworth dates back to Tudor times, although it was rebuilt during the first half of the 18th century. It was reputedly a haunt of highwaymen and a tunnel links it with All Saints' Church, used by smugglers to move their contraband from the vaults of the church to the cellars of the inn.

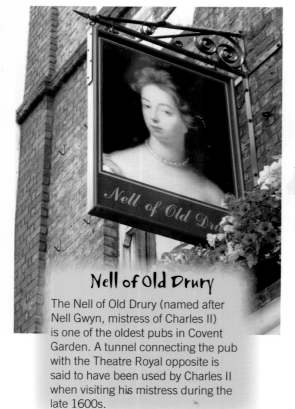

Nell of Old Drury

The Nell of Old Drury (named after Nell Gwyn, mistress of Charles II) is one of the oldest pubs in Covent Garden. A tunnel connecting the pub with the Theatre Royal opposite is said to have been used by Charles II when visiting his mistress during the late 1600s.

Dating from 1890, Gordon's Wine Bar, on Villiers Street, near Embankment Underground station, claims to be the oldest in London. It is based in atmospheric cellars that date back to the late 17th century.

Ye Olde Cheshire Cheese is without question one of London's best-known and well-loved ancient hostelries. It was rebuilt just after the Great Fire of London but there has been a pub on this site for much longer. Many well-known people drank here including Dr Johnson, Voltaire, Charles Dickens and Mark Twain. Its popularity and iconic status is summed up in the book *Piccadilly Jim* by P.G. Wodehouse: 'I've seen all of England … I've seen Westminster Abbey and the Houses of Parliament and His Majesty's Theatre and the Savoy and the Cheshire Cheese.' The cellar, which is part of the pub's drinking area, was once the vault of a monastery's northern gatehouse and the lines of the vault's narrow, pointed arches can still be seen.

London has a rich theatre history, some with underground associations. The Criterion Theatre in Piccadilly Circus, built in 1873, stands on the site of a 17th-century posting inn. The theatre, which is completely below ground, was used to broadcast live programmes by the BBC during the Second World War. Being underground made it an ideal studio and it was safe from the Blitz.

London Bridge Station, built in 1836, is the oldest station in London (the first bridge across the Thames was also built near here). A long row of Victorian railway arches stands underneath the station, most of them in a desperate state of repair. Much of the original stone decoration, however, remains intact and some parts of the labyrinth have become the home to atmospheric venues such as the Southwark Playhouse and the Shunt Lounge.

LEFT:
The impressive entrance to the British Library features a monumental bronze sculpture of Isaac Newton by Eduardo Luigi Paolozzi. The sculpture was inspired by William Blake's famous illustration of the great astronomer.

BELOW LEFT:
The entrance to the underground Criterion Theatre situated on Piccadilly Circus.

The British Library is the world's second largest library (only the US Library of Congress is larger). Twelve million books are stored in four levels of very large basements 23m (75ft) deep, on shelf after shelf in controlled temperatures. The original site has housed in turn a pre-Victorian burial ground, slums, a Zeppelin bomb site and a railway goods station. Rumour has it that the Victoria Line also passes through.

Benjamin Franklin, scientist, diplomat, philosopher, inventor and Founding Father of the United States, lived in London between 1757 and 1775. During the renovation of his home in Craven Street – now a museum – nine human skeletons, six of them children, were found in the basement. These were remnants of the cadavers from the anatomy school housed in the cellar, dating from the time Franklin lived here.

LEFT:
US Founding Father Benjamin Franklin lived in his London house from 1757 to 1775.

Ghosts and Other Stations

ABOVE:
An early London Underground train. The underground railway opened in 1863.

RIGHT:
Art deco archer at East Finchley Station.

The London Underground, which saw the Metropolitan line open for business on 10 January 1863 with 30,000 passengers on the first day, is an engineering marvel. Today it has 270 stations and 407km (253 miles) of track carrying millions of people every year. This all contributes to making the system predictably crowded, claustrophobic and at times uncomfortable. Nonetheless it has given the world the immortal diagrammatic map of the system, originated by Harry Beck in 1932.

It has expressed itself in stations of the highest architectural merit such as Park Royal and East Finchley and the monumental headquarters block of 55 Broadway with its sculptures by Henry Moore and Jacob Epstein. It has produced famous iconic advertising and poster art of the very highest quality. More modestly it has given us the distinctive glazed terracotta station fronts, the colour of oxblood, and the Art and Crafts faience work of the architect Leslie W. Green. These date from the 1900s and many of them can still be seen on the Bakerloo and Piccadilly lines.

BRIGHTEST LONDON
IS BEST REACHED BY
UNDERGROUND

However, 'Underground' is something of a misnomer as only about 40 per cent of the system actually runs below the surface and ….

- the longest escalator at 60m (197ft) is at Angel whilst the shortest is at Stratford
- the deepest lift shaft is at Hampstead at 55m (181ft) and the shortest is Westminster at 2.5m (8ft)
- the most popular route for tourists, as well as the shortest distance between tube stations, is Leicester Square and Covent Garden on the Piccadilly line (0.25km or 0.16 miles)
- the first escalator was introduced at Earls Court in 1911. Wooden-legged Bumper Harris was employed to travel up and down the escalator to prove that it was safe.

The deep-level tunnels played a heroic role in the Second World War, sheltering vast numbers of Londoners (each could hold 8,000 people) during the Blitz. They also provided bomb-proof factories for war supplies, stores for valuable works of art and housed top-secret control centres which played a major influence on the allied war effort.

ABOVE:
Night by Jacob Epstein on the façade of 55 Broadway, London Underground's headquarters.

TOP LEFT:
An example of the iconic art produced for the London Underground posters.

BELOW:
The distinctive logo of London Underground has become a defining part of London's identity.

RIGHT:
The Old Bull
and Bush pub
at Hampstead.

RIGHT:
The Ancient
Greek Elgin
Marbles
were stored
at Aldwych
Station during
the Second
World War.

There is something poignant about stations on which the lights have gone out forever and the Underground system has about 40 'ghost stations' – abandoned or relocated stations. Visible evidence of several of these (Aldwych, York Road, South Kentish Town and Brompton Road) can be seen at street level while some (St Mary's, Whitechapel Road, York Road, British Museum and City Road) show traces of former platforms, which can be seen by those with a quick eye who know where to look as their train speeds through.

Perhaps the most fascinating closed station is one that never opened. The putative North End Station at Hampstead has come to be thought of as Bull and Bush after the famous nearby pub. It was an extremely deep station and was used during the Second World War for the safe storage of vital archives. The only way to get at this material was to make an arrangement for the archivist to travel in the cab with the driver who would then let him off at the uncompleted platform at North End. The feelings of this person as the lighted train rushed away into the tunnel can well be imagined. There were rudimentary lights but, except when trains approached and passed, there was a pervasive, tangible and absolute cold silence and loneliness.

Opened in 1907 as the Strand, Aldwych Station was built on the site of the Royal Strand Theatre and is reputedly haunted by the ghost of an actress, standing where the tracks are now. She is usually seen by cleaning staff at night. During the Second World War it was used as a public air-raid shelter and housed some of the valuable artefacts from the British Museum, including the Elgin Marbles. Today Aldwych is kept as a museum piece and film set.

South Kentish Town was depicted in an atmospheric short story of the same name by Sir John Betjeman about a clerk who mistakenly steps off an Underground train when the doors open in error at a disused station. The train then drives off, leaving the man standing there alone. Confused, he decides to climb the spiral staircase, all 294 steps. As he nears the top he bangs his head on the floorboards of one of the shops above the station. He calls out but no one hears him. The man then descends back down to the platform wondering if he will ever get home. It is a wonderfully eerie story and is reputedly based on a true account.

A particular 'ghost station', which can be seen in the flash of an eye, is the old British Museum Station, opened in July 1900. However, with the opening of Holborn Station in 1906 less than 90m (300ft) away and the amalgamation of the lines under single management in 1933, it was decided to combine the stations. British Museum Station was used as a military administrative office and emergency command post up to the 1960s. Down Street Station opened in 1907 and closed in 1932 because it was never sufficiently busy due to its close proximity to Hyde Park Corner Station. At the outset of war in 1939 it was identified as an obvious choice for an air-raid shelter. Among the occupants of the shelter were the Emergency Railway Committee and Winston Churchill, who nicknamed it 'The Burrow'. The war cabinet used it until the Cabinet War Rooms were ready. Although the platform tunnels are bricked up they can be made out from trains passing between Hyde Park Corner and Green Park.

King William Street, named after the monarch of the time, was built between 1829 and 1835 to provide an approach to what was then the new London Bridge. The station that formerly stood in this street was the City terminus of the City and South London Railway, a line of international historical importance as the world's first successful underground electric railway, opening in 1890 but closing in 1900. *The Railway Magazine* of February 1901 asked whether or not the station and its associated tunnels could be used for the growing of mushrooms.

ABOVE:
The British Museum's Great Court, designed by Norman Forster. The vast foyer beneath the curving glass roof is well served with cafés and is a popular meeting place.

RIGHT:
Aldwych Station, which changed its name from Strand in 1917, still bears the old name outside. It closed in 1944.

The vast underground tunnel that links Bank and Monument Stations is part of one of the largest and most complex subterranean railway stations in the world. Bank Station, named after the nearby Bank of England on Threadneedle Street, was opened in 1900. There had been a proposal to demolish the 18th-century church of St Mary Woolnoth to build the station, but after public protest only the crypt (now the Northern line booking hall) was used. The bodies – it had been used for burials – were moved, the crypt strengthened and the church's foundations underpinned. During the Blitz in January 1941 the station received a direct hit by a bomb which went through the road surface and exploded, killing 56 people and injuring 69.

The station and the Bank of England are famously haunted by the ghost of Sarah Whitehead, the 'Bank Nun' who, grief-stricken at the execution of her brother, loitered near the entrance of the bank every day between 1812 to 1837. There is a drawing of her in the Bank of England Museum.

During the Second World War many people sought shelter in the Underground. The conditions were not particularly pleasant and safety was not assured even within the bowels of London. Twenty people were killed when a bomb hit Marble Arch Station on 17 September 1940. The following month seven were killed at Trafalgar Square when a bomb penetrated the ground and exploded at the top of the escalators, leading to a mudslide which smothered the platforms. In the following two days explosive bombs fell on Paddington Praed Street, and a bomb destroyed the road above one of the Northern line platforms at Balham.

The latter resulted in the road collapsing and a drain fracturing which caused an underground river to bury 68 people beneath a pile of sludge and rubble. Bethnal Green Station was the tragic scene of the worst civilian disaster of the Second World War when 173 people were killed and 92 were injured in a crush whilst attempting to enter the station on 3 March 1943. Eye witnesses testify

to the dreadful suffocation as bodies piled on top of each other and how they heard the groaning and screaming of people being crushed. Above the entrance to the station is a small commemorative plaque, which was placed here in 1993 to the victims of the disaster although moves are afoot to erect a more befitting monument.

Liverpool Street Station stands on the site of the Bethlehem Royal Hospital, founded in 1247. The infirmary first started treating mental patients – hence 'bedlam' – around 1377 although the methods they employed for therapy would strike us today as nothing less than barbaric.

Marble Arch Station has the distinction of being located near to the old Tyburn gallows, where at least 50,000 people met their deaths between the late 12th century and 1783. Countless numbers of bodies of those executed were placed in unmarked burial pits close by and their remains have been unearthed from time to time during building work. It is believed that the body of Oliver Cromwell is among those unceremoniously dumped in one of these pits – minus its head!

No driver, no passengers

Twenty metres (70ft) beneath the streets of London was a railway that ran for 19 hours a day. It carried no passengers and its trains had no drivers or guards, but it was one of the most successful railways in the world. Between 1927 and 2003 the London Post Office Railway (Mail Rail) carried mail from Paddington Head District Sorting Office to Eastern Head District Sorting Office at Whitechapel.

TOP:
Concerts were often organized in an attempt to keep spirits up.

ABOVE:
The Mail Rail: containers of mail being loaded ready for their journey in 1928.

ABOVE:
The Woolwich Foot Tunnel offered an alternative to the ferry.

RIGHT:
Congestion on the Woolwich Ferry. By 1933, 16,000 vehicles used the ferry each week.

Kingsway was built in the early 1900s to ease congestion and to help to eliminate some of London's most notorious slum areas. A year after the completion of Kingsway, the Kingsway Tram Tunnel, running 9m (31ft) under the road, opened in 1906, extending to the Victoria Embankment in 1908. The last trams ran in London in April 1952 when the tunnel closed. From 1964–84 part of it was converted into a traffic underpass.

Tower Subway is not strictly part of the Underground system but was the world's first underground railway. It consists of an iron tube, 2m (7ft) in diameter and 376m (1,235ft) in length, laid 6m (18ft) below the bed of the River Thames. A single carriage train, operated by cable, was used as a shuttle service between the two banks of the river in 1870. Unfortunately the railway was only open for less than four months and had to close because of poor patronage.

Beneath the Thames

There are at least 20 tunnels running beneath the River Thames. These include three disused and nine used London Underground tunnels, two BT tunnels, three road tunnels, two foot tunnels and eight service tunnels, which carry mainly water supplies, telephone and electricity cables.

LEFT:
A notice on the Greenwich Foot Tunnel reminds users not to cycle.

There is a plethora of pedestrian passageways – underpasses or subways – in London. Whilst the majority run under busy roads there are notable ones that run under the Thames. Opened in 1912, the Woolwich Foot Tunnel in south-east London offered pedestrians an alternative way to cross the river when the Woolwich Ferry service was not running – bad winter fogs often prevented it from operating. The tunnel was dug by hand; it is 504m (1,655ft) in length and the top is 3m (10ft) below the river bed. It was used by thousands of workers in the Royal Docks, at one time the main employers of North Woolwich and Silvertown. About 5km (3 miles) further down river is the Greenwich Foot Tunnel which runs under the Thames between Cutty Sark Gardens at Greenwich and Island Gardens on the Isle of Dogs. At over 366m (1,200ft) long and approximately 15m (50ft) deep, it was designed by Sir Alexander Binnie and opened in 1902.

The first tunnel to be successfully constructed under a navigable river was the Thames Tunnel connecting Rotherhithe and Wapping, built between 1825 and 1843 by Marc Brunel, father of the more famous Isambard Kingdom Brunel. By the early 19th century, with London's traffic congestion growing, a demand emerged for the construction of more bridges, which helped to relieve the problem. Construction of the Thames Tunnel proved to be extremely dangerous with flooding as well as foul air in the tunnel which caused fevers. When it was opened to foot traffic on 25 March 1843 it was hailed as the eighth wonder of the world. However, despite it being a triumph of civil engineering (396m or 1,300ft long and 23m or 75ft below the river's surface), the Thames Tunnel cost a fortune to build and was not a financial success.

Visitors to the Kensington museums will be familiar with the long tunnel that leads from South Kensington Station. After the success of the Fisheries Exhibition of 1883 and the Health Exhibition of 1884 the tunnel was built and a toll of one penny was charged. Other exhibitions followed and in 1908 it was opened permanently, free of charge.

ABOVE:
The Thames Tunnel under construction in 1830. This ambitious project to tunnel 4.3m (14ft) below the deepest point of the River Thames was begun by Marc Brunel and completed by his son Isambard Kingdom Brunel.

Water, Water Everywhere

Ask most people which river flows through London and the answer will be the Thames; some might add the Lea. Today it is difficult to imagine the many rivers that provided fish and fresh water running through the meadows and fields of pre-urban London into the Thames. Centuries ago Londoners would have been familiar with many rivers. A number of London localities started their existence as small villages along these rivers and their place names reflect their origin. The course of the rivers formed valleys where houses and roads developed, along with drains, sewers and industries.

What happened to these rivers? As London developed and expanded beyond its city wall into the outlying villages, the rivers gradually became buried. Thousands of people who walk the London streets are unaware that they are walking above water. The routes and contours of many of the rivers can still be followed and at times they have become fleetingly visible. In 1941 a German bomb hit Oxford Street and the River Tyburn could be seen through the bottom of the crater.

London's largest subterranean river is the Fleet – on early maps and illustrations of London it is quite distinctive. The river rises in Hampstead and joins the Thames near Blackfriars Bridge. In medieval times, the Fleet was navigable as far as

Holborn and provided a useful trade route into the City. Tanneries and slaughterhouses lined the banks of the Fleet where the dyes and blood turned the river various shades of red. Jonathan Swift gave a typically vivid picture of the Fleet and how it was a depository for all types of filth: 'Seepings from butcher's stalls, dung, guts and blood, drown'd puppies, stinking sprats, all drenched in mud, dead cats and turnip-tops come tumbling down into the flood.' Pollution had plagued the river from at least the 14th century despite a number of efforts to clean it. During the 17th century the river became notoriously filthy and deteriorated into an obnoxious open sewer. So repugnant and polluted was the 'abominable sink of nastiness', it was covered over in 1766 from Fleet Street to the Thames. By the 1870s the river disappeared in its upper reaches beneath the new suburbs of Hampstead and Kentish Town.

The River Tyburn (not to be confused with the nearby Tyburn Brook) runs from South Hampstead into the Thames near Vauxhall Bridge. Like many of the Thames' tributaries that crossed central London, the Tyburn became the course for a sewer – a far cry from when its clear water was appreciated for its purity and provided excellent sport for anglers. In 1900 engineers who were constructing the Central line or 'Tuppenny Tube' found problems with the Tyburn because water from it kept penetrating the workings. In 1875 workmen building a sewer in Stratford

Place unearthed a structure of stone which was probably the first reservoir in London, built around 1237 to store water from the Tyburn – which was then piped to the Great Conduit in Cheapside and other locations to provide a water supply for the City of London.

Despite being lost for over five centuries, the River Walbrook has given its name to a ward, a street and a church. Its name derives from the fact that the river was a brook that ran through the Roman wall. It was an important river to the Roman settlement of Londinium, shown by the building of a temple to the god Mithras on the east bank. The Walbrook's transition from a 'fair brook of sweet water' in the 12th and early 13th centuries to an open sewer by the late 13th century was confirmed when its lower reaches were covered in order to make it free from 'dung and other nuisances'.

The Westbourne rises in Hampstead Heath as several streamlets and flows into the Thames near the Royal Hospital Chelsea. The Serpentine in Hyde Park, which was formed in 1730, was fed with the Westbourne's waters until 1834, by which time it had become too polluted.

South of the river, the Effra, from the Celtic word for torrent, once flowed from Norwood to Vauxhall as an open stream, but as Lambeth expanded and became urbanized, the river was covered and turned into a sewer in the 1850s. It is the longest of South London's rivers.

About 800m (half a mile) to the east of Tower Bridge on the south bank of the Thames is a small inlet, at one time used by barges loading and unloading at the nearby wharves and warehouses. This inlet, often called St Saviour's Dock, is actually the mouth of a short stream called the Neckinger which rises in Southwark, close to the place where the large and important Cluniac monastery of Bermondsey Abbey once stood. The river gets its curious name from the fact that River Thames pirates were once executed here and the rope that was used to do the job was known as the 'Devil's neckcloth' or 'neckinger'.

All of London's canal tunnels are on the Regent's Canal, which stretches from Paddington to Limehouse, a distance of 13km (9 miles). One famous incident occurred in 1874 when a barge carrying an inflammable and volatile cargo of loose gunpowder in sacks and barrels of petroleum caused an explosion, destroying Macclesfield Bridge, killing three men and a horse. There are three tunnels along the canal: Islington, Maida Hill and Eyre's. The route through the tunnels was first operated by 'legging', which involved men lying on their backs aboard the boat and walking the vessel through the tunnel against the side-walls. This method was not without its risks. In 1825 a boat was being legged through Maida Hill tunnel when the planks on which the men were lying slipped. Two men died, one was severely injured, whilst a third body was never found.

ABOVE:
Barges on the Grand Union Canal. In 1929 the Regent's Canal and Grand Junction Canal became part of the expanded Grand Union Canal. However, by this time commercial use was in decline.

LEFT:
The body of the pirate William Kidd, who was executed in 1701, was left to hang in an iron cage for 20 years as a warning to other pirates. A pub of the same name stands on the waterside at Wapping.

The Great Stink

Mysterious underworld

As people walk around the capital most are oblivious to the many buildings, dummy façades, disguised ventilation shafts and entrances that lead to an underworld of tunnels, bunkers and control centres. For example, the unusual doors at the base of Boudicca's statue near Westminster Bridge lead to utility subways which run to Blackfriars and the Bank of England. An electricity sub-station beneath Leicester Square is entered by a disguised trap door to the left of the Half Price Ticket Booth, a structure that also doubles as a ventilation shaft.

THE "SILENT HIGHWAY"-MAN.
"Your MONEY or your LIFE!"

RIGHT:
In 1849 it was discovered that contaminated water in the River Thames was the cause of the virulent disease cholera among the city's population. This cartoon appeared in *Punch* magazine.

Before the 16th century most Londoners depended on the River Thames or one of its springs or tributaries for their water supply. In 1236 the Tyburn Conduit conveyed water from what is now Oxford Street to Cheapside via Piccadilly, the Strand and Fleet Street. The building of London's water supply dates from the Great Fire (1666) which destroyed the previous networks. Several waterworks companies were established in the 18th century.

The main problem was contaminated water, which physician John Snow discovered in 1849 as the cause of cholera. It took two Acts of Parliament to make sure that London would be provided with 'pure and wholesome water'. The quality of drinking water improved as a result of advances in the treatment and supply of water.

RIGHT:
A rat catcher at work in the sewers, 1861.

Most of London's water network is underground and much of the water piping is still cast-iron piping dating back to the 19th century, although this is gradually being replaced.

In *Hubbub: Filth, Noise and Stench in England*, Emily Cockayne quotes a contemporary Londoner in 1726 faced with drinking from the Thames which, he comments, 'is impregnated with all the filth of London and Westminster – human excrement is the least offensive part of the concrete, which is composed of all the drugs, minerals and poisons, used in mechanics and manufacture, enriched with the putrefying carcasses of beasts and men; and mixed with the scourings of all the wash-tubs and kennels and common sewers, within the bills of mortality'. London's sewers were open ditches that sloped slightly to drain human wastage toward the River Thames, and ultimately into the sea. By the 18th century most houses had cesspits that often flooded through the floorboards. Even the best of homes could have a nauseating stench permeating the parlour.

With the huge increase in population, and the problems of disposing of sewage, London faced an environmental catastrophe by the mid-19th century. When the 'Great Stink' of the summer of 1858 became too much to bear for Members of Parliament, they were finally driven to deal with the problem. In addition to the smell was the danger presented by water-borne diseases such as cholera. For the next seven years Joseph Bazalgette (1819–91), Chief Engineer to London's

further downstream. This meant that large mud banks formed and the incoming tides brought it back in – which was highlighted in a terrible accident in 1878. The pleasure cruiser SS *Princess Alice*, carrying 750 people, collided with a steam collier ship, the *Bywell Castle*. The *Alice*, a much smaller ship, took four minutes to sink to the bottom of the river. The majority of passengers had to cling to the bits of flotsam left over from the collision and wait for rescue, at the same time that an outfall sewer pumped thousands of gallons of raw sewage into the river. The toxic pollution was disfiguring and it made rescuing and identifying the people a terrible task. In 1882 a Royal Commission recommended chemical treatment of the sewage.

Underground places continue to fascinate, give rise to speculation, and evoke curiosity as well as fear. Thoughts of entering deep dark tunnels, not knowing where they might lead or what one might find, has provided a rich seam of fiction for literature, TV and film. London's 'underground' holds many secrets, as well as revealing much about the city's colourful and rich history.

ABOVE:
Deepening the Fleet Street sewer in 1845.

LEFT:
Victorian decorative ironwork at the Abbey Mills Pumping Station, East London.

BELOW:
The collision in 1878 of the *Bywell Castle* with the smaller SS *Princess Alice*, which sank in only four minutes.

Metropolitan Board of Works, designed a huge sewage disposal system for the capital, including the intercepting sewers, pumping stations and outfall sewers.

Bazalgette's achievement was extraordinary: London was provided with over 2,000km (1,300 miles) of sewers. However, there was the problem that the sewage was disposed of

Rats a-roaming

Today Thames Water provides a network of 351 sewage treatment works and 64,374km (40,000 miles) of sewers. At some points the tunnels open up into large chambers. Maintaining such an extensive system includes scraping the deposits of fat and grease inside the drains and poisoning rats. For example, workers once took eight weeks to clear a 46-m (150-ft) solidified mass of hardened fat with pick axes from sewers underneath the Leicester Square area. Although much of the inspection work is carried out by remote controlled machines that carry cameras and lights, there is a small, dedicated team of Thames Water workers who have to perform tasks that machines still cannot.

Walk A: The South Bank

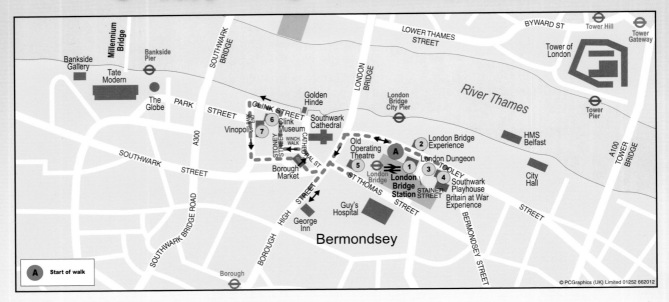

Starts and ends at London Bridge Underground. Distance: 1.6km (1 mile)

1 The London Dungeon

Turn right out of the main entrance of the Underground station on to Tooley Street and a short distance down the road is The London Dungeon. The dungeon has been located under London Bridge Station since 1976 and the sound of trains overhead adds to the atmosphere. It offers a grisly history of plague, torture and executions. It stands on the site of a 16th-century pillory and a 'cage' which was used to keep disorderly people who were arrested too late in the day to be imprisoned.

2 The London Bridge Experience and London Tombs

Directly across the road is The London Bridge Experience which tells the story of London Bridge through the ages. It is housed in the excavated tombs and catacombs, which date from the time of John Rennie's bridge of 1831, now in Arizona. The tunnels were originally used for warehousing and were sealed off for decades. Visitors can also visit the scary London Tombs, built from a series of excavated 14th-century plague pits.

3 London Bridge Arches

Walk further along Tooley Street, away from the station. Running parallel to the south of Tooley Street is St Thomas Street. Between these streets are the elevated tracks of London Bridge Station (the oldest station in London, first opened in 1836), under which there is a multitude of alleys and rooms. One of the intersecting streets, Stainer Street, was bombed when people were sheltering under the arch during an air raid in the Second World War. Sixty-eight people died and 175 were injured: there is a plaque at the St Thomas Street end.

4 Southwark Playhouse

Walk as far as the junction with Bermondsey Street. On the right-hand side is Southwark Playhouse which is below London Bridge Station. George Orwell stayed in a doss-house on Tooley Street where he wrote notes for *Down and Out in Paris and London*. Also on the right is the Britain at War Experience which recreates the London Blitz and has an underground cinema playing wartime newsreels. Walk back along Tooley Street and Duke Street Hill as far as London Bridge.

5 The Old Operating Theatre Museum

Turn left along Borough High Street as far as St Thomas Street, which is on the left. A few steps along here is The Old Operating Theatre Museum where the gory sights of yesteryear's surgery can be seen. Retrace your steps back to Borough High Street where a little further south you can enjoy a drink at The George, the oldest galleried coaching inn in London. Cross the road and head towards Borough Market – a great food market well worth a visit. Cross Cathedral Street towards Southwark Cathedral. Walk around the cathedral towards the river, left along Winchester Walk and right up Stoney Street to the *Golden Hinde* and into Clink Street.

6 The Clink Prison Museum

The Clink Prison Museum is on the site of the original Clink Prison, in the basement of a former warehouse. The prison held prisoners from the early Tudor years until 1780. The name of the Clink is the origin of the phrase 'in the clink' (in prison), as well as reflecting the noise of the prisoners' chains. At the end of Clink Street turn left.

7 Vinopolis

Vinopolis, a visitor attraction dedicated to the enjoyment of wine, is at 1 Bank End, under the massive Victorian viaduct arches, built in 1866 to carry an extension line from London Bridge Station over the Thames to the north bank. Here you can enter the cellars for a wine-tasting experience. A fee is charged for the tour.

Retrace your steps to London Bridge Underground.

Walk B: The City of London

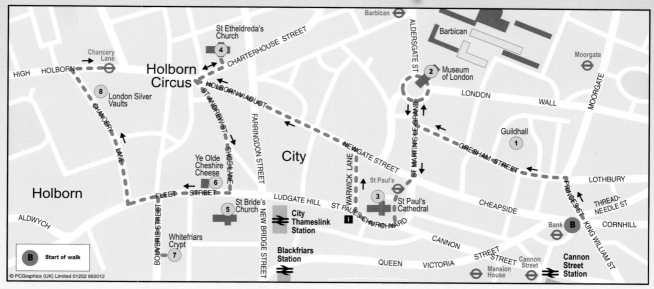

Starts at the Guildhall, Gresham Street (nearest Underground is Bank) and ends at Chancery Lane, which is also the nearest Underground. Distance: 3.2km (2 miles)

1 Guildhall
Make your way from Bank Underground station up Prince's Street, left on Lothbury which becomes Gresham Street. The Guildhall is on your right. The capital's only Roman amphitheatre is entered via the art gallery on the lower ground floor. There is a small admission fee. The amphitheatre was used for the entertainment of soldiers and the public, with animal fights and public executions of criminals. Immediately beneath the Guildhall itself is the crypt, the most extensive medieval one in London.

2 Museum of London
Turn right along Gresham Street until you get to Aldersgate Street. Turn right to London Wall where you will find the Museum of London, the world's largest urban history museum. The remains of the west gate of the city wall can be seen beneath the streets next to the museum. Admission is free.

3 St Paul's Cathedral
Walk back south along Aldersgate Street and then St Martin's Le-Grand, and St Paul's Cathedral, Wren's masterpiece, will come into view. The crypt of St Paul's is the largest in Western Europe. An admission fee is charged to enter the cathedral.

4 St Etheldreda's Church Crypt, near Hatton Garden
Walk away from the cathedral west along St Paul's Churchyard, taking the first right up Warwick Lane to the end. Turn left along Newgate Street and Holborn Viaduct. At Holborn Circus turn first right into Charterhouse Street. Ely Place is a cul-de-sac on the left. St Etheldreda's is the oldest Catholic church in England and contains an attractive crypt.

5 St Bride's Church
Walk back to Holborn Circus, take the second left down St Andrew Street then Shoe Lane, until you reach Fleet Street. Almost opposite is St Bride's, the journalists' church. Take note of the beautiful Wren spire which is said to inspire wedding cakes. The crypt is well worth a visit.

6 Ye Olde Cheshire Cheese
Turn right and walk west along Fleet Street. On the right-hand side is Ye Olde Cheshire Cheese, a famous old London pub along Wine Office Court. Rebuilt in 1666, the vaulted cellars are thought to belong to a 13th-century Carmelite monastery which once occupied the site. Many famous people including Dr Johnson, Pepys, Dickens, Tennyson and Conan Doyle have drank here. Go downstairs into the cellars and enjoy a drink or a meal.

7 Whitefriars Crypt
Continue west along Fleet Street, looking out on the opposite side for Bouverie Street. Walk down as far as Magpie Alley on the left. At the end of the alley is a small court – look over the railings to see the remains of the Whitefriars crypt. This crypt, thought to date from the late-14th century, is the only visible remains of the medieval Carmelite priory.

8 London Silver Vaults
Retrace your steps to Fleet Street, turn left and continue west as far as Chancery Lane on the north (right) side of the street. Towards the end of Chancery Lane on the right are the London Silver Vaults with three floors underground. They were opened in 1876 to provide strong rooms for the treasures of London's wealthy elite.

Continue right up Chancery Lane and right along High Holborn to reach Chancery Lane Underground.

Walk C: Westminster

Starts at Westminster Underground and ends at Piccadilly Circus Underground. Distance: 1.6km (1 mile)

1 Westminster Abbey

From Westminster Underground, cross Bridge Street and walk around to the far corner of Parliament Square. Go down Broad Sanctuary to the front of Westminster Abbey. This has been the coronation church since 1066 and is the final resting place of 17 monarchs. The present church, begun by Henry III in 1245, is one of the most important Gothic buildings in the country. The Pyx Chamber is a low vaulted room off the East Cloister. A museum is housed in the magnificent vaulted undercroft beneath the former monks' dormitory and is one of the oldest areas of the abbey. The centrepiece is the collection of royal and other funeral effigies.

2 Churchill Museum and Cabinet War Rooms

From Broad Sanctuary, walk north along Storey's Gate until you get to Horse Guards Road just over Great George Street. On the right is the Churchill Museum and Cabinet War Rooms located beneath the Treasury. The Cabinet War Rooms, a remarkable underground complex, were used as an operational command centre by the British Government throughout the Second World War. Churchill slept in a small bedroom – although this only amounted to three nights over the course of the war.

3 Site of Henry VIII's Wine Cellar – Ministry of Defence

Turn right into King Charles Street and left at Parliament Street, which becomes Whitehall. On the right is the Ministry of Defence, which is not open to the public. This is where the old Whitehall Palace once stood (it burned down in 1698), and the only remaining feature is Henry VIII's wine cellar.

4 Benjamin Franklin House

Continue north up Whitehall towards Trafalgar Square and turn right on to Northumberland Avenue then left into Craven Street. The museum, at number 36, is the world's only remaining home of Benjamin Franklin, a United States Founding Father. The house was built around 1730 and it holds a Grade I listing. It also retains many original features, including the central staircase, 18th-century panelling, stoves, windows, fittings, beams and bricks.

5 St Martin-in-the-Fields Crypt

Retrace your steps back to Trafalgar Square where St Martin-in-the-Fields Church is at the far right-hand corner. The entrance to the crypt and café is on the north side of the church. The present church was designed by James Gibbs and completed in 1726, and has become one of the most significant ecclesiastical buildings in the English-speaking world. Excavations at the site in 2006 led to the discovery of a grave dated about AD 410.

6 Gordon's Wine Bar

Walk along Duncannon Street on the south side of the church towards Charing Cross Station. Turn left along the Strand and

take the first right turn after the station into Villiers Street. Along here is Gordon's Wine Bar, recognizable by its 'olde worlde' look. Go down the stairs to the cellar. Possibly the oldest wine bar in London, the building in which the bar is situated was home to Samuel Pepys in the 1680s.

7 Criterion Theatre

Retrace your steps to Trafalgar Square, along Cockspur Street opposite, right up Haymarket and north to Piccadilly Circus where the underground Criterion is prominently located near the Eros statue. The theatre was built on the site of a 17th-century coaching inn. The present building was opened in 1873 with a performance of *The American Lady*.

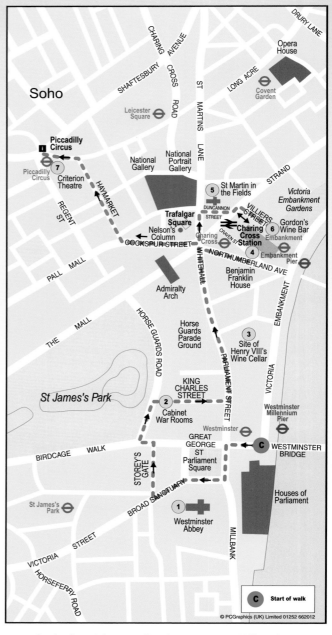

Gazetteer

Admiralty Citadel
Horse Guards Parade
Underground: Westminster and
St James's Park
Admission free

Bank of England Museum
Bartholomew Lane, off Threadneedle
Street
www.bankofengland.co.uk/education/
museum
Underground: Bank and Monument
Admission free

Benjamin Franklin House
36 Craven Street
www.benjaminfranklinhouse.org/
Underground: Charing Cross and
Embankment
Admission charge: under £10

Berry Brothers & Rudd
3 St James's Street
www.bbr.com
Underground: Green Park
Open for wine tastings and events

The British Library
96 Euston Road
www.bl.uk/
Underground: King's Cross and St
Pancras
Admission free to permanent exhibition
gallery. By ticket to special exhibitions.
Readers must apply for a (free) pass.

Brompton Cemetery
Fulham Road
www.royalparks.org.uk/parks/brompton_
cemetery/
Underground: West Brompton
Admission free – donation of £4 for the
guided tour

The Brunel Museum
Railway Avenue, Rotherhythe
www.brunel-museum.org.uk/
Underground: Canada Water
Admission charge: under £10

Bunhill Fields
City Road
www.quakerinfo.com/bunhill.shtml
Underground: Old Street
Admission free

**Churchill Museum and Cabinet War
Rooms**
King Charles Street
www.cwr.iwm.org.uk
Underground: Westminster and
St James's Park
Admission charge: over £10, free for
children under 15

Christ Church Spitalfields
Fournier Street
www.spitalfieldsvenue.org/
Underground: Liverpool Street
The crypt is not open to the public but
admission to the church is free (tours
carry a charge)

The Clink Prison Museum
1 Clink Street
www.clink.co.uk
Underground: London Bridge
Admission charge: under £10

Criterion Theatre
Piccadilly Circus
www.criterion-theatre.co.uk/
Underground: Piccadilly Circus
Admission: by ticket for a show

Ginglik
Shepherd's Bush Green, Shepherd's
Bush
www.ginglik.co.uk
Underground: Shepherd's Bush
Admission to members only

Gordon's Wine Bar
47 Villiers Street
www.gordonswinebar.com/
Underground: Embankment and
Charing Cross
Admission free

Guildhall
Gresham Street
www.guildhall.cityoflondon.gov.uk/
Underground: Moorgate, Bank,
Mansion House and St Paul's
Entry to the Roman amphitheatre
is included in the admission to the
art gallery
Admission charge less than £10

Highgate Cemetery
Swain's Lane
www.highgate-cemetery.org/
Underground: Archway
Admission: under £10

Hop Exchange
24 Southwark Street
www.hopexchange.co.uk/
Underground: London Bridge
Open for hire as a venue only

**Huggin Hill Roman Bath House
Remains**
Huggin Hill
Queen Victoria Street
Underground: Mansion House
Admission free

Bank of England

St Bartholomew the Great

St Martin-in-the-Fields

Lambeth Palace
Lambeth Palace Road
www.archbishopofcanterbury.org/108
Underground: Lambeth North
Lambeth Palace is not open to the
general public though tours can be
arranged by writing to the bookings
department.
Form available from www.
archbishopofcanterbury.org/941

The London Apprentice
62 Church Street, Old Isleworth
www.thelondonapprentice.co.uk
Underground: Richmond
Admission free

**The London Bridge Experience and
London Tombs**
2–4 Tooley Street
www.thelondonbridgeexperience.com
Underground: London Bridge
Admission charge: over £10

The London Dungeon
28–34 Tooley Street
www.thedungeons.com
Underground: London Bridge
Admission charge: over £10

The London Silver Vaults
53–64 Chancery Lane
www.thesilvervaults.com
Underground: Chancery Lane
Admission free

London Transport Museum
Covent Garden Piazza
www.ltmuseum.co.uk/
Underground: Covent Garden
Admission charge: around £10

The Mason's Arms
Upper Berkeley Street
www.fancyapint.com/pubs/pub1123.html
Underground: Marble Arch
Admission free

Merrill Lynch
King Edward Street
www.ml.com
Roman remains are open to the public by
appointment only

The Morpeth Arms
55 Millbank
www.pubs.com/pub_details.cfm?ID=211
Underground: Pimlico
Admission free

Museum of London
150 London Wall
www.museumoflondon.org.uk/English/
Underground: Barbican
Admission free

Nell of Old Drury
Catherine Street
www.nellofolddrury.com/direct.htm
Underground: Covent Garden
Admission free

The Old Operating Theatre Museum
9a St Thomas Street
www.thegarrett.org.uk
Admission charge: under £10

Ye Olde Cheshire Cheese
Wine Office Court, Fleet Street
www.pubs.com/pub_details.cfm?ID=216
Underground: Blackfriars
Admission free

Southwark Playhouse
Shipwright Yard (corner of Tooley Street
and Bermondsey Street)
www.southwarkplayhouse.co.uk/
Underground: London Bridge
Admission: by ticket for a show

Spaniards Inn
Spaniards Road, Hampstead Heath
www.pubs.com/pub_details.cfm?ID=240
Underground: Hampstead
Admission free

St Andrew Holborn
5 St Andrew Street
www.standrewholborn.org.uk
Underground: Chancery Lane and
Farringdon
Admission free

St Bartholomew the Great
West Smithfield
www.greatstbarts.com/
Underground: Barbican and St Paul's
Admission charge: under £10

St Bride's Fleet Street
www.stbrides.com/
Underground: St Paul's and Blackfriars
Admission free

St Clement Danes
Strand
www.raf.mod.uk/stclementdanes/
Underground: Temple
Admission free

St Etheldreda's
14 Ely Place
www.stetheldreda.com/home.html
Underground: Chancery Lane and
Farringdon
Admission free

St Martin-in-the-Fields
Trafalgar Square
www.stmartin-in-the-fields.org
Underground: Charing Cross and
Leicester Square
Admission free

Highgate Cemetery

Leicester Square

Berry Bros & Rudd

St Mary le Bow
Cheapside
www.stmarylebow.co.uk
Underground: St Paul's, Mansion House
and Bank
Admission free

St Paul's Cathedral
St Paul's Churchyard
www.stpauls.co.uk/
Underground: St Paul's
Admission charge: over £10

Temple of Mithras
Queen Victoria Street
Underground: Bank and Mansion House
Admission free

Tower of London
Tower Hill
www.hrp.org.uk/toweroflondon/
Underground: Tower Hill
Admission charge: over £10

Viaduct Tavern
Newgate Street, Smithfield
http://www.fancyapint.com/pubs/pub156.
html
Underground: St Paul's
Admission free

Vinopolis
1 Bank End
www.vinopolis.co.uk/
Underground: London Bridge
Admission charge: over £10

Westminster Abbey
Victoria Street
www.westminster-abbey.org
Underground: St James's Park and
Westminster
Admission charge: over £10

Whitefriars Crypt
Freshfields, Bouverie Street
Underground: Blackfriars
The crypt is visible from outside. Turn off
Fleet Street down Bouverie Street and look
out for Magpie Alley on the left
Admission free

Blackfriars Bridge

Abbey Mills Pumping Station

St Paul's Cathedral

Green Park

47

MAP KEY

1. Admiralty Citadel
2. Bank of England Museum
3. Benjamin Franklin House
4. Berry Bros & Rudd
5. The British Library
6. Brompton Cemetery
7. The Brunel Museum
8. Bunhill Fields
9. Churchill Museum and Cabinet War Rooms
10. Christchurch Spitalfields
11. The Clink Prison Museum
12. Criterion Theatre
13. Ginglik
14. Gordon's Wine Bar
15. Guildhall
16. Highgate Cemetery
17. Hop Exchange
18. Huggin Hill Roman Bath House Remains
19. Lambeth Palace
20. The London Apprentice
21. The London Bridge Experience and London Tombs
22. The London Dungeon
23. The London Silver Vaults
24. London Transport Museum
25. The Mason's Arms
26. Merrill Lynch
27. The Morpeth Arms
28. Museum of London
29. Nell of Old Drury
30. The Old Operating Theatre Museum
31. Ye Olde Cheshire Cheese
32. Southwark Playhouse
33. Spaniards Inn
34. St Andrew Holborn
35. St Bartholomew the Great
36. St Bride's Fleet Street
37. St Clement Danes
38. St Etheldreda's
39. St Martin-in-the-Fields
40. St Mary le Bow
41. St Paul's Cathedral
42. Temple of Mithras
43. Tower of London
44. Viaduct Tavern
45. Vinopolis
46. Westminster Abbey
47. Whitefriars Crypt

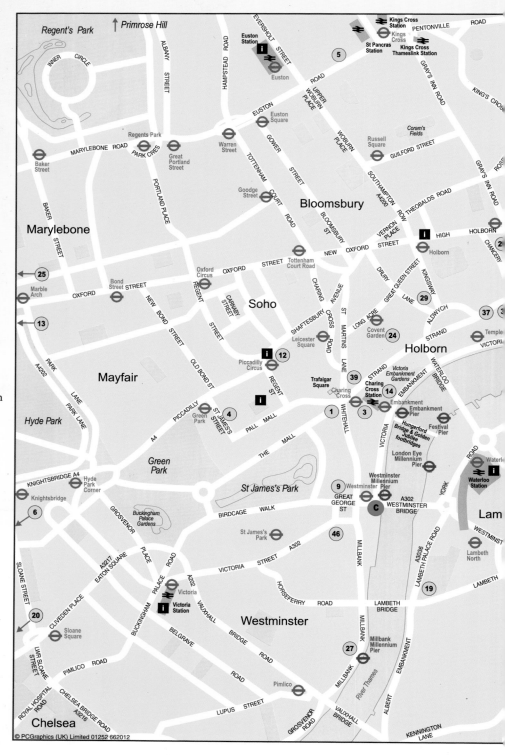

© PCGraphics (UK) Limited 01252 662012